M000111266

infuse

Christmas
light splits the night

by Diane Averill
and Amy Brown

FAITH
ALIVE®
Christian Resources

Grand Rapids, Michigan

*"Do not be afraid.
I bring you good news that will
cause great joy for all the people.
Today . . . a Savior has been born to you;
he is the Messiah, the Lord."*
—Luke 2:10-11

We are grateful for the many comments and helpful suggestions of interested small groups and leaders who contributed to the development of this study.

Lesson 1 of this study was first pilot-tested as a Christmas lesson titled "The Prophets Foretold" and was made available for download by Christian Reformed Home Missions small group ministries (www. smallgroupministries.org). Diane Averill wrote the lesson material, and Amy Brown wrote the Break Away readings for that lesson. The authors adapted the lesson to be included in this study. Lessons 2 and 3 and the Leader's Notes (available for download at www.faithaliveresources.org) for this study are written by Diane Averill, and the Introduction and Lessons 4 and 5 are written by Amy Brown.

Cover photo: Bigstock

Map: Matthew P. Faber

Printed in the United States of America.

We welcome your comments. Call us at 1-800-333-8300 or email us at editors@faithaliveresources.org.

ISBN 978-1-59255-513-0

Contents

Map: Judea in Jesus' Day 4

Glossary 5

How to Use This Study 8

An Invitation and Prayer of Commitment 9

Introduction 10

Lesson 1
A Light in Deep Darkness 12

Lesson 2
Meet the Relatives 22

Lesson 3
A Scandal? A Stable? Shepherds? 34

Lesson 4
Don't Be Afraid: Good News and Peace! 44

Lesson 5
Celebrate—the King Is Coming! 54

Evaluation Questionnaire

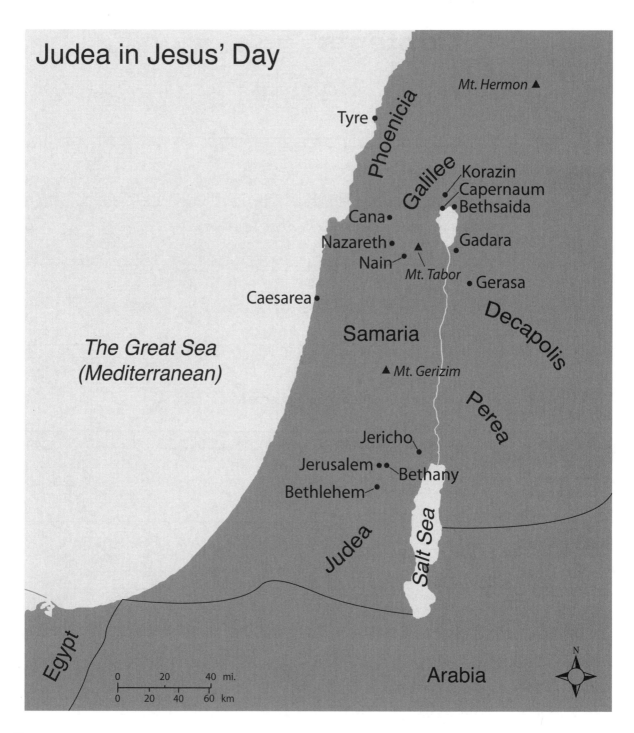

Judea in Jesus' Day

Mt. Hermon ▲

Tyre ●

Phoenicia

Galilee

Korazin
Capernaum
● Bethsaida

Cana ●

Nazareth ●
Nain ●
▲
Mt. Tabor

Gadara

● Gerasa

Decapolis

Caesarea ●

Samaria

▲ Mt. Gerizim

The Great Sea
(Mediterranean)

Perea

Jericho ●
Jerusalem ●● Bethany
Bethlehem ●

Salt Sea

Judea

Egypt

Arabia

N

0   20   40 mi.
0   20   40   60 km

4

Glossary

Abraham—father of the Jewish people (Israel), renowned for his faith in God's promises (Gen. 12:1-7; 15:6; Heb. 11:8-16). Also called "the father of all who believe" in Christ (Rom. 4:11).

angel(s)—supernatural beings created by God to be messengers, to carry out God's will in this world, and to serve and care for all who belong to God (Ps. 91:11-12).

angel of the Lord—This figure appears at times to God's people (often as a man) to make announcements or judgments in God's name (see Gen. 16:7; 22:11-18; Josh. 5:13-15; Judg. 6:11-12; 13:2-23). Sometimes this angel is also referred to as "the Lord" (for example, see Gen. 16:13; Judg. 6:14), and the *NIV Study Bible* explains that "as the Lord's personal messenger who represented him and bore his credentials, the angel could speak on behalf of (and so be identified with) the One who sent him." (See also Ex. 23:20-23.)

Babylon—main capital of the Babylonian Empire (614-539 B.C.), which ranged from the Persian Gulf to Egypt and north into part of Asia Minor (modern Turkey). The Jews became subject to Babylon in 605 B.C., and Jewish royalty and influential families were exiled. Another deportation took place in 597 B.C. in which about 10,000 soldiers, smiths, and officials were exiled. Babylon conquered and destroyed Jerusalem in 586 B.C. and scattered more of the Jews around the empire. After another deportation in 582 B.C. the estimated total of Jewish exiles was about 70,000. (See 2 Kings 24-25; 2 Chron. 36; Esther 2:5-7; Dan. 1:1-5.)

Caesar Augustus—ruler of the Roman Empire at the time of Christ's birth. Augustus was the first caesar to rule over Judea (31 B.C.-A.D. 14), and he conducted his first census when Jesus was born (Luke 2:1).

Christ—see **Jesus Christ**, **Messiah**.

David—Israel's greatest king in the Old Testament. The Lord promised that one of David's descendants would rule faithfully on his throne forever (2 Sam. 7). As Matthew 1 shows, Jesus Christ is that "Son of David."

disciple—a follower; one who is taught. This term refers commonly to followers to Jesus.

exile—The people of Israel were exiled because of their sin against God. After King David's son Solomon died, the nation split into a northern kingdom (ten tribes) and a southern kingdom (two tribes). The northern kingdom was conquered and exiled by the Assyrian Empire in 722 B.C. (2 Kings 17). The southern kingdom was overtaken by the Babylonian Empire and exiled in several deportations (2 Kings 24-25; 2 Chron. 36). See also **Babylon**.

faith—defined in Hebrews 11:1 as "being sure of what we hope for and certain of what we do not see." Can be defined in simple terms as "belief and trust." True saving faith is a gift that consists of knowledge and confidence—a sure knowledge by which we accept as true all that God has revealed in his Word, and confidence that all our sins are forgiven in Jesus' name through his death on the cross as our Savior.

the Father—the first person of the Trinity. The other two persons are God the Son (Jesus Christ) and God the Holy Spirit. They are three persons in one being.

favor—God's merciful grace to us. See **grace**, **mercy**.

Galilee—the Roman province in northern Palestine where Jesus grew up.

Gentiles—all people who are not Jews.

good news—see **gospel**.

gospel—literally means "good news" and refers to the message of God's salvation from sin and the promise of eternal life through Christ.

grace—God's undeserved favor and forgiving love. Jesus is the full expression of God's grace for the salvation of all who believe in him as Lord and Savior (Eph. 2:8-10).

holy—pure; set apart to bring glory to God.

Holy Spirit—the third person of the Trinity. The other two persons are God the Father and God the Son (Jesus Christ). They are three persons in one being. The Holy Spirit convicts us of sin, works true faith in our hearts, and empowers us to live holy lives. The Spirit's presence in our hearts guarantees that we will receive God's promises (John 16:7-15; Rom. 8:11; Eph. 1:13-14).

hope—in combination with faith this means looking ahead in solid trust to the fulfillment of all God's promises (see Heb. 7:19; 11:1).

Isaac—Abraham and Sarah's son, who inherited all the promises God made with Abraham.

Isaiah—a Hebrew prophet from around 700 B.C. who foretold the coming of Christ (Messiah) and described his service and suffering.

Jacob—Isaac's son whom God renamed Israel (Gen. 32:28) and who became the patriarch of the twelve tribes of Israel.

Jerusalem—Israel's historic capital city. As the location for God's temple, it became the center for the Jewish religion and the spiritual headquarters of the nation of Israel.

Jesus Christ—the sinless Son of God, who gave his life as the payment for our sin. *Jesus* means "Savior," and *Christ (Messiah)* means "Anointed One." He is the second person of the Trinity. The other two persons are God the Father and God the Holy Spirit. They are three persons in one being. See also **Messiah**.

Jews—the people of Israel, descendants of Abraham; God's special people chosen to be a blessing to all other nations (Gen. 12:2-3).

Jordan—a river running through Palestine from the Sea of Galilee to the Salt Sea (Dead Sea).

Joseph—a carpenter from Nazareth in Galilee whom God chose to be the husband of Mary and the adoptive father of Jesus.

kingdom of God—God's rule over all things, especially evident in the lives of his people, who follow Jesus and believe in him as Savior.

Mary—a young virgin whom God chose to be the mother of Jesus, conceived through the Holy Spirit (Matt. 1:18-20; Luke 1:26-38).

mercy—God's free and undeserved compassion. To be more precise, it refers to showing leniency by holding back punishment even if justice calls for it (see Mic. 7:18-19).

Messiah—the promised deliverer of God's people. Both the Hebrew word *Messiah* and the Greek word *Christ* mean "Anointed One." Through the prophets God promised to send the Messiah, the Savior-King, to deliver his people from oppressors and to rule in righteousness forever. The people misunderstood those promises, however, and looked for a Messiah who would be a political ruler and gather an army to rout all physical enemies (see John 6:15; Acts 1:6). But as Jesus revealed through his work and teaching, the Messiah came to save God's people from the oppression of sin and death and to give them new life forever with God. He rules today in heaven at the right hand of the Father, and when he comes again at the end of time, he will fully establish God's everlasting kingdom of righteousness on earth. (See Matt. 26:63-64; John 16:5-16; 1 Cor. 15; Rev. 21:1-5; 22:1-5.)

Naphtali—with Zebulun (Isa. 9:1), one of the northern tribes of ancient Israel that were first to be conquered and exiled by the Assyrian Empire in 722 B.C. (See 2 Kings 17.) See also **exile**.

Nazareth—a small town in the province of Galilee where Jesus grew up.

peace—a result of salvation through Jesus Christ (reconciliation with God) that yields an assurance of well-being and freedom (guided by the Spirit) to live wholly in relationship with God and others. (See John 14:26-27; Rom. 5:1-11; Eph. 2:13-22; Phil. 4:4-9.)

prophet—someone who speaks God's message (see Deut. 18:17-19); generally a person who preached God's Word and (in some cases) foretold the future as revealed by the Lord.

righteous—considered right with God; sometimes this term is used to describe a person of upright character who strives to honor God (Matt. 1:19; see Gen. 6:9; 15:6; Job 1:1). As God's people, we are called to be righteous and are credited with Christ's righteousness: we are made right with God through Jesus' death and given the ability to live in right relationships with others through the power of the Holy Spirit (Rom. 3:21-26).

salvation—deliverance from oppressors; ultimately, salvation in the Bible refers to deliverance from our slavery to sin. Jesus came to save all who believe in him as Savior from the curse of sin and death, so that we can be reconciled with God, given the righteousness of Christ, and have new life forever with God. (See John 3:16; 8:34-36; Rom. 3-8.)

sin—disobedience to God; refers to breaking God's law (1 John 3:4).

Spirit (Holy Spirit)—see **Holy Spirit**.

Zebulun—see **Naphtali**.

Zion—another name for the city of Jerusalem (ancient Jebus), conquered by David, which later became the center of worship for God's people Israel. In David's day, it was known as the fortress of Zion (the meaning of the name is unknown). (See Judg. 19:10; 2 Sam. 5:6-7; Ps. 2:6; 9:11.)

How to Use This Study

This Bible study aims to help people engage in lively discussion and learning without having studied the text before doing each lesson together.

Map, Glossary
Near the front of this booklet are a map and glossary that can be useful for locating places and the meanings of terms mentioned in the Scriptures for this study.

Questions for Discussion
The main questions for discussion are numbered and are in bold print. Along with these questions you'll find points "to think about as you discuss" to help spark ideas for responding to each main question. In addition, you'll often see questions that help to connect the story to everyday life under the subheading "What does this mean to me?"

Please do not feel you have to answer every question in the lesson material. Our goal is to help make Bible study a creative, flexible, exploratory exercise in which you engage with your group and grow to know God and each other better.

Follow-up Ideas
At the end of each lesson are Explore! ideas that you might like to use for follow-up. These include activities that can help you learn more about items of interest related to the lesson and apply your learning to everyday life. There are also music and video suggestions.

Break Away (at-home readings)
After the study material for each lesson you'll find readings for use at home. Take a break with God and do some thinking about the lesson material and how the Lord can use it to shape your life. If you like, clip these pages out and set them in places around your home or at work where they can remind you to spend time with God. You might also like to memorize some of the Scriptures used in these pieces.

An Invitation and Prayer of Commitment
If you're searching for a relationship with God, or studying with a friend who is searching, see An Invitation (to believe and commit to God) and a Prayer of Commitment provided on the next page of this booklet. These can be helpful in talking one-to-one with God or with someone who is ready to make a faith commitment to God.

Leader's Notes
At the Faith Alive website page featuring this Bible study—visit www.FaithAliveResources.org, search for "Infuse Christmas," and click on the link to "Leader's Notes"—you'll find tips for leading this small group study.

We wish you God's blessing as you participate in Bible study together. Have fun as you learn and grow closer to God and one another!

The following invitation and prayer tools may be helpful to you in approaching God or in helping someone else do so.

An Invitation

Listen now to what God is saying to you. Maybe you are aware of things in your life that keep you from coming near to God. Maybe you have thought of God as someone who is unsympathetic, angry, and punishing. You may feel as if you don't know how to pray or how to come near to God.

"But because of his great love for us, God, who is rich in mercy, made us alive with Christ even when we were dead in transgressions—it is by grace you have been saved" (Eph. 2:4-5). Jesus, God's Son, died on the cross to save us from our sins. It doesn't matter where you come from, what you've done in the past, or what your heritage is. God has been watching over you and caring for you, drawing you closer. "You also were included in Christ when you heard the word of truth, the gospel of your salvation" (Eph. 1:13). Do you want to follow Jesus? It's as simple as A-B-C:

- **A**dmit that you have sinned and you need God's forgiveness.
- **B**elieve that God loves you and that Jesus has already paid the price for your sins.
- **C**ommit your life to God, asking the Lord to forgive your sins, nurture you as his child, and fill you with the Holy Spirit.

Prayer of Commitment

Here is a prayer of commitment recognizing Jesus as Savior. If you want to be in a loving relationship with Jesus Christ, pray this prayer. If you have already committed your life to Jesus, use this prayer for renewal and praise.

Dear God, I'm sorry for the wrong and sinful things that I've done. I need your forgiveness. I know I need Jesus as my Savior, and I know you listen to sinners who are truthful to you. Please forgive me and help me to live in a right relationship with you.

Thank you, Jesus, for dying on the cross to pay the price for my sins. Father, please take away the guilt that I feel because of my sin, and bring me into your presence. Thank you, Lord, for loving me and saving me.

Holy Spirit of God, help me to pray, and teach me to live by your Word. Help me to follow you faithfully. Make me more like Jesus each day, and help me to share your love and good news with others everywhere. In Jesus' name, Amen.

Introduction

What comes to mind when you think of Christmas? Gifts and mistletoe? Family parties and high-calorie treats? Decorated stores and Santa Claus? It can seem odd that the origin of such a glittering holiday is in the birth of a child long ago, whose arrival had none of the comforts and pleasures we connect with Christmas today. That baby boy was born in a cattle stall over two thousand years ago, and his first bed was the animals' feed trough (a manger).

Of the countless babies born in this world, what was so special about this one? Several hundreds of years before his birth, prophets had foretold that a child would be born who would deliver God's people and rule the nations of the earth with justice. This baby would become a king, but not just any king—this baby was actually the Son of God himself in human form: King of kings, Lord of lords, Savior of the world.

That's how Jesus Christ, the Savior-Messiah, came to us—a tiny baby who grew into a person like no other in history. It is his birth we celebrate on December 25. His birth inspired decorations in the shapes of stars and angels, and it prompted much of the music we hear only at this time of year. Each Christmas season, with its parties and decorations and singing, gives us an opening to remember the strange and wonderful time when light split the night and God became one of us.

Advent—Participating in Christ's Coming

Advent is the season of preparation in which Christians around the world ready their hearts and homes for the celebration of Christ's birth. It begins on the fourth Sunday before Christmas and ends on Christmas Eve. When Christmas Eve falls on a Sunday, it is considered to be the fourth Sunday in Advent, with Christmas Eve itself beginning at sundown.

Many churches and families count down the weeks of Advent by using an Advent wreath. This circular wreath (often made with evergreens) sits on a table and holds five candles—four in a circular pattern, and a fifth, called the Christ Candle (usually white), at the center. Each week a candle is lit (one the first week, two the second, and so on), and on Christmas Eve all

In churches of the Western tradition, begun in Rome, **Advent** marks the beginning of the new church year and is celebrated with the use of an Advent wreath (below).

of the candles are lit, including the Christ Candle. Candles of any color that reminds people of Christmas may be used. Some traditions call for four red or blue candles surrounding a white one. Many Advent candle sets come with three purple candles, one pink candle, and a white candle for the center. The purple can represent preparation as well as Christ's royalty or his passion (suffering on the cross); the pink can represent joy; and the white usually represents purity and light. If you decide to use these colors, the order often used is purple for weeks one and two; pink for week three; purple for week four; and white for Christmas Eve—and then, optionally, all candles lit again on Christmas Day.

In addition to the colors of the candles, there is a theme for each week. Again, this may vary with different traditions. In this study the themes we will be using are hope, love, joy, and peace, and then the last candle symbolizes the celebration of Christ's birth.

This study follows the traditional four weeks of Advent as a guide for developing greater joy and anticipation for the wonder-filled Christmas season. The fifth lesson then includes a celebration of Christ that looks ahead to his second coming, so you may want to plan a party (see p. 54)!

Optional ideas to consider before you begin:

- Make or buy an Advent wreath for your group. Each week, begin your session by having someone in the group lead the Advent Wreath exercise, reading aloud the brief Advent Scripture and Advent reading, lighting the candle(s), and leading the group prayer. The group may also wish to sing the suggested Christmas carol.
- To create anticipation for your Christmas study, send out holiday-themed invitations. These can be made easily and inexpensively on a computer or with craft paper and are a wonderful way to invite someone new.
- Christmas cookies, cocoa, mulled cider, or other traditional holiday treats are a delicious part of the Advent season. Plan ahead and ask group members to take turns bringing in their favorites each week. On the final week you'll want several people to participate with the celebration! (See p. 54.)
- Some lessons include optional craft projects in the Explore! section that follows the discussion questions. With a little preparation, these can make for a fun addition to your Bible study!

Lesson 1
A Light in Deep Darkness

Isaiah 9:1-7

From the prophecy of Isaiah we learn of a special child to be born. This child would be like no other; his life and death would change all of history. As we read, some of the places and historical references may be unfamiliar, but the emotions and experiences are timeless. Consider how these verses speak to us today as we recognize the hope we have received in Christ.

Opener (optional)
Many people have conflicting emotions about the Christmas season. Describe some of the emotions you experience during this holiday.

Isaiah 9:1-2
Isaiah was a prophet (740-681 B.C.) who wrote about the present and the future. He challenged and advised the kings of Israel that ruled during his lifetime. To those who had turned away from God, he offered a voice of judgment; to God's faithful people, who were living in uncertain times, he offered a voice of hope and comfort. In this passage Isaiah prophesied about an eternal kingdom to be ushered in by the birth of a special child.

1. What are some of the contrasting images in these two verses? Why do you think Isaiah used them?
To think about as you discuss . . .
  • to whom Isaiah was speaking
  • what his words would have meant to them

Advent Wreath (Optional)

Week One—Hope
Read: Isaiah 7:14

We light this first candle of Advent remembering the **hope** the prophets and the people had that someday a special child would be born.

Group prayer: Thank you, God, that you fulfilled the hopes of your people when you sent your Son into the world as a baby. Thank you that because he came, we can have hope as well. Amen.

Christmas carol: "Come, Thou Long Expected Jesus"

See the glossary for information on the place names in this passage of Isaiah.

FLASHBACK

A fulfilled prophecy (Isa. 9:1–2)—here Isaiah speaks to the most northern of Israel's tribal groups, Zebulun and Naphtali, who were the first to fall in the Assyrian invasions of the eighth century B.C. Through the prophet, God promises that these territories, now "walking in darkness," will be the first to see "a great light." Matthew 4:13–17 shows that Jesus fulfilled this prophecy as he began his teaching and healing ministry in Galilee.

In John 8:12 Jesus declares, "I am the light of the world. Whoever follows me will never walk in darkness, but will have the light of life."

2. What kind of emotional atmosphere do the people of Israel seem to be living under?

To think about as you discuss . . .
- words in the passage that communicate emotion
- changes that would take place

hope—in combination with faith this means looking ahead in solid trust to the fulfillment of all God's promises (see Heb. 7:19; 11:1).

3. What hope does this passage offer to people in Isaiah's day? How about in our day?

To think about as you discuss . . .
- why hope is important
- how this hope will come, and what it looks like

What does this mean to me?
- How can this light and the hope it brings make an impact in your Christmas celebrations this year?

Isaiah 9:3-5

4. What are the feelings expressed in these verses, and what are the reasons for these feelings?

To think about as you discuss . . .

- how God's promises bring us hope
- what freedom and peace look like
- implications of the burning of warriors' boots and battle garments

5. What are some events or experiences that would cause you to express yourself in the way the Israelites did?

To think about as you discuss . . .

- how God has taken care of you
- a time of blessing in your life (perhaps a joyful Christmas memory)

What does this mean to me?

- If you knew there would be no more war, how would your life be different?

6. What are some kinds of "yokes" people put on themselves?

To think about as you discuss . . .

- how the Christmas season can become a burden
- expectations we put on ourselves
- expectations others put on us

The word **advent** means "coming" or "arrival," especially in reference to something important. During this season we anticipate with joy the past arrival of the infant Jesus, who came to save us from our sins (Matt. 1:21). We also look forward to Christ's Second Advent, when he will come again at the end of time.

Isaiah 9:6

7. From the statement here, how would you describe the child to be born?

8. What comes to mind as you reflect on the titles for this child?
Use the following Scriptures to expand your thoughts:
- Wonderful Counselor (Rom. 11:33-34)

- Mighty God, Everlasting Father (John 1:1-3)

- Prince of Peace (Rom. 5:1-11; Eph. 2:13-22)

If there's time, see also Isaiah 11:1-9 and note similarities you find . . .

Isaiah 9:7

9. What type of government is described here?
To think about as you discuss . . .
- words and phrases that show this government is different from others
- the positive results of this government
- who and what brings it about

A Son Called Father?
Though Jesus, as the Son of God, is not to be confused with God the Father, scholars note that in his role as our provider and protector in saving us from sin, the Son born to us is rightly called Everlasting Father. Just as "God so loved the world that he sent his one and only Son" (John 3:16), so the Son loves us so much that he came to save us (see Phil. 2:6-8).

For a helpful reference about "**David's throne**," see Luke 1:26-33, where we read of an angel speaking to Mary about the birth of Jesus. Other information comes from the genealogies of Jesus in Matthew 1 and Luke 3, which we'll cover in lesson 2.

10. Picture a place where justice and righteousness are established forever. What would it be like in this place?

To think about as you discuss . . .
- how it would be to live in complete safety
- what it would be like with no injustice or prejudice
- how people would treat one another

As you think about these possibilities, you may want to **reflect on Revelation 21:1-7**.

What does this mean to me?
- How does this picture of life give us hope as we celebrate the Christmas season?

More to Think About

- In all of your hopes for the Christmas season this year, how can you focus more intently on the hope described in Isaiah 9:1-7?

- Consider these words from Ephesians 2:12-14: "Remember that . . . you were separate from Christ . . . without hope and without God in the world. But now in Christ Jesus you who once were far away have been brought near through the blood of Christ. For he himself is our peace . . . ." What emotions does this passage evoke in you? Why?

- Has the Christmas season been a burden to you in the past? Make a list of your expectations (can you think of ten or more?), and then read through them, taking a few moments to think about each one. How many are truly necessary for a peaceful and hope-filled Christmas?

Explore!
(optional activities to do with your group or on your own)

- As a follow-up to this lesson, listen to Handel's *Messiah*, a musical feast in the Christmas season. The refrain known as "For Unto Us a Child Is Born" is based on verses from Isaiah 9:1-7. (Find it on www.youtube.com by searching "Messiah For unto us a child.")
- Consider getting involved in a cause that looks ahead in hope to the coming of God's kingdom in its fullness. Check with health, welfare, political action, denominational, and environmental agencies for ideas and help in getting started. Be creative! Follow the Lord's leading to do something that can make an impact for Christ in your community and beyond.
- **Craft idea!** The Christmas star is often used as a symbol of hope. A beautiful ornament can be made by constructing a Moravian (or German) star out of simple strips of paper. Websites with detailed instructions can be found online. Just type "how to make paper German star" in your Internet browser search area. Hang your completed star in a place where you can see it often—and pause to think about the hope that Christ offers you this Christmas season.

Break Away (at-home readings)

God Keeps His Promises
All this took place to fulfill what the Lord had said through the prophet: "The virgin will conceive and give birth to a son, and they will call him Immanuel" (which means "God with us").

—Matthew 1:22-23

The "prophet" whom Matthew is referring to is Isaiah, who wrote about the coming of Immanuel ("God with us") about seven hundred years before his birth (see Isa. 7:14). This was a promise pointing to the Messiah of God's people (see glossary), and those centuries made for a long, hard wait for the people of Israel.

Often it seems as if God waits a long time to answer our prayers, and we might wonder if he even hears them. Is there something in your life that you have been praying about for a long time? Are there prayers you have stopped asking, because you've given up hope of receiving an answer? (Don't give up. God always hears us, and he is faithful. But he is also God; he doesn't always answer in the way we might want or expect. See Isa. 55:6-7; Matt. 6:5-15; Acts 2:21; James 1:5; 4:3; 5:16; 1 John 4:14-15.)

Christmas is a season of hope. Matthew 1:22-23 points to the reason why. God's people prayed for a very long time, keeping their faith alive in the hope that God heard them and would answer. When he did answer, it was in a far greater way than his people imagined (see Eph. 3:20-21). Instead of coming to save only them, the Lord came as a tiny baby with the power and desire to save all people who would call out to him. His answer included us!

Take a few minutes to think about some prayers God has answered in your life. If you are using a journal, write them down. Thank the Lord for the work he has been doing in your life.

Where in your life do you need hope? Ask God for help with that, and ask him to build your faith by rekindling your hope.

Longing for Righteousness

"'At that time I will make a righteous Branch sprout from David's line; he will do what is just and right in the land. In those days Judah will be saved and Jerusalem will live in safety. This is the name by which it will be called: The Lord Our Righteous Savior.'"

—Jeremiah 33:15-16

Righteousness is the condition of being right with God, and it connects closely with justice being done in all kinds of relationships. In this broken world, sadly, unrighteousness seems to flourish more than righteousness does. But wherever the Lord is at work in us and in this world, we can find evidence of righteousness, justice, peace, and goodwill.

During the Christmas season people often do many things to try to lift the burdens of those who suffer because of the unrighteousness of others—gifts are given to children of prison inmates, money is sent to women's shelters, cards are sent to soldiers overseas. There is a longing, a hope, within each of us for a world that is completely just and righteous.

That desire comes from God. We have been born into a broken world, and we ourselves are so broken that, on our own, it is impossible to please God by what we do. Our hope can only be in "The Lord Our Righteous Savior," who can transform us from being part of the problem to part of the solution.

Meditate on these words from 1 Corinthians 13:4-8:

> Love is patient, love is kind. It does not envy, it does not boast, it is not proud. It does not dishonor others, it is not self-seeking, it is not easily angered, it keeps no record of wrongs. Love does not delight in evil but rejoices with the truth. It always protects, always trusts, always hopes, always perseveres. Love never fails. . . .

Ask yourself, are you loving toward others? Toward your family? Toward the person in the checkout line? Toward the person who cuts you off in traffic? Toward the person begging for change on the street corner? Toward your new or annoying next-door neighbor? Do you even know your neighbors? Righteousness and justice start in our hearts, changing the world around us, wherever we are.

Ask God for the strength and desire to bring his kingdom into the communities in which you live. This Christmas season, what is *one* thing you can do to bring God's righteousness and love to people around you?

God's Eternal Tenderness

"Here is my servant, whom I uphold, my chosen one in whom I delight; I will put my Spirit on him, and he will bring justice to the nations. . . . A bruised reed he will not break, and a smoldering wick he will not snuff out. . . . In his teaching the islands will put their hope."
—Isaiah 42:1-4

This sketch of Jesus (also used in Matt. 12:18-21) is not usually what we picture when we think of someone who has the authority to "bring justice to the nations." Why do you think God chose to send the world this kind of deliverer?

God's kindness, says Romans 2:4, is intended to lead us to repentance. He is patient with us, "not wanting anyone to perish, but everyone to come to repentance" (2 Pet. 3:9). How do these descriptions of God contrast with the ways people often view God?

How do your thoughts and behaviors portray Christ to others? If you were the only picture of Christ that someone ever saw, what would they think God thought of them?

"God is *love*," says the apostle John in 1 John 4:8. Meditating again on 1 Corinthians 13:4-8, we can read the passage this way, substituting *love* with *God*, whose identity is *love*:

> God is patient, God is kind. He does not envy, he does not boast, he is not proud. God does not dishonor others, he is not self-seeking, he is not easily angered, he keeps no record of wrongs. God does not delight in evil but rejoices with the truth. God always protects, always trusts, always hopes, always perseveres. God never fails . . . .

Serving this God gives us hope. Ask the Spirit of God to give you a clearer picture of his tenderness and love toward you and toward the people around you.

Humble Beginnings

"But you, Bethlehem Ephrathah, though you are small among the clans of Judah, out of you will come for me one who will be ruler over Israel, whose origins are from of old, from ancient times."

—Micah 5:2

Bethlehem, a tiny, unimportant town in Israel, became the center of the world on the night Christ was born. No worldly king would have chosen such an ignoble place for his son.

Why do you think God seems to love humble, unworthy things? What is it about humble, unnoticeable people that makes them attractive to God?

Take a few minutes to meditate on the humility of Christ's birth—the tiny town, the teenage mother, the barn or stable in which he was born (see Luke 2:7—his mother "placed him in a manger," a feed trough for livestock). Contrast this with the expectations placed on Christmas in our culture today. What is one way you can bring some of this humility back into your Christmas celebration?

Meditate on the power of God that used such a humble beginning to change the world's history. Are there any places in your life where you feel small, weak, or defeated? Ask God to empower you by his Spirit to turn them into places where you can see his hand at work in your life.

Living an Examined Life

"The thief comes only to steal and kill and destroy; I have come that they may have life, and have it to the full."   —John 10:10

The season of Advent (anticipating Christmas) is a good time to take stock of your life. A good place to start is by asking God to examine your life. According to Richard Foster in his book *Prayer*, there are two things to reflect on when we do this. The first is to become aware of how God has been present to us during our day and how we have responded to him. The second is to allow God to bring to our attention those areas that need his cleansing, purifying, and healing.

Today, as you rest in God's presence, invite the Holy Spirit to examine your heart. Pray as David did in Psalm 139:23-24: "Search me, O God, and know my heart; test me and know my anxious thoughts. See if there is any offensive way in me, and lead me in the way everlasting."

Christ came not so that we would feel condemned for our many shortcomings (see John 3:17). He came so that we can have life to the full. When you think of a full life, what do you see? How do you think a full life brings glory to God? Why is it important to be aware of how you are living your life?

The message the prophets spoke was a song of hope. Christ is that hope. Meditate on the work he is doing right now in your life. Thank him for the things he is doing, and ask him to do more!

Lesson 2
Meet the Relatives

Matthew 1:1-17; Luke 3:23-38

The genealogies or lists of Jesus' ancestors in Matthew 1 and Luke 3 are provided to establish his family line. In the Jewish culture it was important to know a person's ancestry, especially if that person came from a royal line. The family tree of Jesus contains the names of many kings and other noteworthy people in Israel. We'll look closely at a few of them in this lesson, and you may want to learn more about them and others at home.

Mary, the mother of Jesus, is also mentioned in the genealogy in Matthew. She is perhaps the most well-known woman in history. But she is not the only woman mentioned—and in those days it was highly unusual to include women's names in a genealogy. As we "meet the relatives" of Jesus, it will be interesting to consider why Matthew listed other women in Jesus' family tree.

Opener (optional)
Have you explored your own ancestry? If so, what have you learned? Why do you think ancestry is important to people today?

EPISODE 1

Matthew 1:1
1. How is Jesus described in verse 1? Why are these details significant?
To think about as you discuss . . .
- what it means to be a "son of David" (see 2 Sam. 7)
- what it means to be a "son of Abraham" (see Gen. 12:1-3; 17:1-16)
- the names *Jesus* ("Savior") and *Messiah* (or *Christ*—"Anointed One")—see glossary

Who was Matthew?

Matthew, the writer of the first book of the New Testament in our Bibles, was a disciple of Jesus. He wrote an account of Jesus' life to share the gospel ("good news") of salvation through Jesus and to present Jesus clearly to the Jews as their Messiah (promised deliverer). That's probably the main reason he included a genealogy of Jesus at the beginning of his book—along with many references to the way Jesus fulfilled prophecies from the Jewish Scriptures (the Old Testament) that pointed to the Messiah.

Before he met Jesus, Matthew worked as a tax collector for the Roman government, the oppressors of the Jewish people at that time. As a tax collector, Matthew, also called Levi, would have been hated as a traitor and a thief. Tax collectors often charged much more in taxes than the Romans demanded—and then pocketed the rest. So they often became very rich (see Luke 19:1-10). In Matthew 9:9-13 and Mark 2:13-17, you can read about how Matthew became a disciple of Jesus.

Matthew 1:2-6

2. **Read through the list of names here (don't worry about how to pronounce them). Comment on names that may be familiar. Note also that women are not usually mentioned in Jewish genealogies. Why do you think Matthew would include them?**

For a fun presentation of the names, listen to a song by Andrew Peterson on www.youtube.com (search "Andrew Peterson – Matthew's begats").

To think about as you discuss . . .
- the patriarchs of Israel (if you're familiar with Genesis)
- names repeated from Ruth 4:18-22
- the four women mentioned in these verses
- what the women have in common (see box on next page)

What does this mean to me?
- What does the inclusion of these women tell us about how God views people?

- What does this show us about how we should view others?

Five Women You Need to Know

- **Tamar**, a Gentile (non-Jew), had to pose as a prostitute to get her father-in-law Judah to perform his marital duties (described by God's law in Deut. 25:5-6). See Genesis 38.
- **Rahab**, a Gentile and a prostitute, helped two spies sent by Joshua to spy out the land promised to Abraham's descendants (Josh. 2).
- **Ruth**, a Gentile from Moab, followed her mother-in-law to live in Bethlehem, where she met and married Boaz (book of Ruth).
- **Bathsheba**, married to a Gentile (Uriah the Hittite), became pregnant by King David while her husband served in the king's army. David had the man killed in battle to cover up this affair. The child, however, died, and David confessed his sin (see Ps. 51). Later Bathsheba gave birth to another son, Solomon, who inherited the throne from his father, David (2 Sam. 11-12; 1 Kings 1-2).
- **Mary**, the wife of Joseph and the mother of Jesus. Mary's own pregnancy was scandalous (see Matt. 1:18-23).
        —adapted from Marilyn A. McGinnis, *Matthew: One King to Rule Them All* (Infuse series, Faith Alive, 2010)

Matthew 1:6b-11

3. This section is about a line of kings. Which names or other details draw your attention?

To think about as you discuss . . .

- again, note Solomon's mother (see 2 Sam. 11-12)
- the lives of Solomon, Rehoboam (see 2 Chron. 1-12)
- details about the other kings (see 2 Chron. 13-36)

"Exile to Babylon" (Matt. 1:11)
After about 605 B.C., because of their disobedience, God punished the Jewish people by giving them over to Nebuchadnezzar of Babylon, who took the royalty and officials and up to 70,000 others in several deportations to exile in Babylonia (see 2 Chron. 36:15-20; Esther 2:5-7; Dan. 1:1-5). The Jewish people were exiles in Babylon for about seventy years (2 Chron. 36:21-23).

4. What interrupts the succession of kings?

To think about as you discuss . . .

- see box about exile to Babylon
- what this tells us about the people of Israel

Babylonian sculpture

Numbers and Genealogies

For thousands of years people have been intrigued by genealogies, and some genealogists have developed number patterns to lend special significance to their subject. For example, the numbers 3, 7, 10, 12, and 40 often take on special meaning as numbers of completeness or perfection. Like many of the Jewish people, who developed a system of number values for names, called *gematria* (based on values assigned to letters in their alphabet), Matthew apparently enjoyed number symbolism. In 1:17 he notes that "there were fourteen generations . . . from Abraham to David . . . from David to the exile . . . and . . . from the exile to the Messiah." Commentators add that the number value for the name *David* is 14, and that the genealogy in Matthew is made up of 3 sets of fourteen, which is twice 7. They also reason that in this way Matthew super-emphasized Jesus' identity as the promised Son of David to draw the attention of many Jews who needed to hear his story. Matthew's many references to the fulfillment of Old Testament prophecies in Christ also support this reasoning.

Today many people are interested in finding out about their relatives from earlier times, if possible. Learning about your relatives through family records, discussions with older family members, and genealogies of various kinds can be a fascinating exercise. Discovery of your "DNA markers" can even tell you what part of the world your ancestors came from centuries or millennia ago. Helpful information about ancestry is available on websites such as www.Ancestry.com, www.RootsWeb.com, www.MyHeritage.com, www.GenealogyLinks.com, and www.WorldRoots.com.

Matthew 1:12-17

5. Considering the descriptions of other men in the genealogy, what is unusual about the way Joseph is noted? Why?

To think about as you discuss . . .

- "how the birth of Jesus . . . came about" (Matt. 1:18; see also Luke 1:26-35)

> **As a matter of fact**, of the four gospel writers who wrote about the life of Jesus (Matthew, Mark, Luke, and John), only Matthew and Luke wrote about his birth, and both listed a genealogy.

EPISODE 2

Luke 3:23-38

6. What does verse 23 tells us about Jesus?

To think about as you discuss . . .

- when Jesus began his ministry
- what we know about Joseph

7. Read through the genealogy in these verses and compare it with the one in Matthew.

Remember not to worry about the pronunciation of names!

To think about as you discuss . . .

- what's different about the order of names listed
- differences in some of the names
- reasons why Luke and Matthew might have different lists (see box about the two genealogies)

8. What new things have you learned from looking at the genealogies in Matthew and Luke?

To think about as you discuss . . .

- what the differences in the genealogies tell us about the writers and their perspectives
- what this tells us about Jesus and his ancestors
- the people and styles God uses to tell his story

Comparing Matthew's and Luke's Lists

Jewish genealogies were very important, and they were kept with great accuracy. It's obvious that Matthew and Luke produced different genealogies. For one thing, the order is different. Matthew's genealogy traces Jesus' lineage forward from Abraham to Jesus, while Luke's traces the lineage from Jesus all the way back to Adam. That gives us two perspectives, with one genealogy being much longer than the other.

There are also differences in the names where we'd expect them to match. Why? We aren't told. But interpreters have offered some helpful explanations.

Some scholars suggest that in Joseph's lineage there may have been a levirate marriage; for example, if Joseph's biological father had died, Joseph's mother and her children could have been absorbed into the household of his father's brother or closest male relative, and then considered the son of that relative. Something like that happened in the case of Obed (Ruth 4; see also Gen. 38:6-11; Deut. 25:5-6; Matt. 1:5; Luke 3:32).

Others suggest that perhaps Matthew wished to trace the legal lineage of the house of David, naming only heirs to the throne; while Luke wished to present a natural lineage, tracing the direct bloodline.

Still others suggest that Matthew used Joseph's line and Luke used Mary's line without mentioning Mary by name. In line with this theory, they note that Luke's phrase "so it was thought" (Luke 3:23) brings to mind the unique occurrence of the virgin birth (Luke 1:26-35).

More to Think About

- Think about your own family background, with its imperfect people. How have you seen God work in your family history despite flaws and weaknesses?

- Consider how God used all types of people in Jesus' family line. How might this be a source of encouragement to you?

- Think about a family member who has been a positive influence in your life. Describe your appreciation for that person. Have you let them know? If not, think of a way you can show them.

Explore!

- Read the book of Ruth. The famous German writer Johann von Goethe called it the greatest short story ever written. Even though Ruth was from the pagan nation of Moab, God worked in her life and she became the great-grandmother of King David. Note also that the mother of Boaz, who married Ruth, was Rahab (see Josh. 2; Matt. 1:5).
- As you sing or listen to Christmas carols this season, take note of references to some of the people mentioned in Jesus' family line.
- Begin recording a family history by talking with an older member of your family. Ask questions about their experiences growing up. Write it down and give them a copy. You may also wish to share the story with your group.

Break Away (at-home readings)

God of Miracles
(working with Abraham and Sarah)

Sarah said, "God has brought me laughter, and everyone who hears about this will laugh with me." . . . "Who would have said to Abraham that Sarah would nurse children? Yet I have borne him a son in his old age." —Genesis 21:6-7

Surprising pregnancies are not uncommon in the Bible, and Sarah, an ancestor of Jesus, experienced one. Well past the age of childbearing, Sarah and Abraham had given up on having a child. But God was and remains the God of miraculous surprises.

Though Abraham and Sarah were flawed individuals, God used them in mighty ways. Even though they did not wait for God but chose to have a son by Sarah's servant (Gen. 16), God still provided the true heir, Isaac, in their old age (Gen. 21). In fact, when they were reminded that this would happen although they were already old, it was so improbable that they both laughed (Gen. 17:17; 18:12). Sarah's surprising pregnancy showed that God can bring babies into this world outside the usual way. Women past childbearing age and even a virgin can become pregnant, if it is in God's plan.

How much do we think about God's plan in our lives, and how that connects to the miraculous? We know that God gives us promises, just as he made promises to Abraham and Sarah. But does God work miracles in our lives? Perhaps we don't see or hear of miracles often, but then maybe we don't have our eyes of faith open to them. God works in many ways, often mysterious and often (what we might call) miraculous. God works behind the scenes, and he works out in the open. Do we see it? Often when miraculous events took place in Bible times, some people recognized them for what they were, but many others didn't.

This Christmas, consider asking God to help you see his work in your life—and to be able to recognize how amazing (miraculous?) it is. Maybe you need to pray for a change in character for yourself or for someone close to you, a change that will make you or that person more like Christ (2 Cor. 3:18; Phil. 2:5). That's an ongoing work of God that is undeniably miraculous! Yet it often takes place quietly and behind the scenes.

Think about Abraham and Sarah again. What was the miracle in their story? Was it the birth of a promised son at their ages of 100 and 90 (Gen. 17:17)? Was it the promise itself? Or that God fulfilled it? Or that God spoke to them and had been at work in their lives? All of the above?

Praise God today for his mighty works, seen and unseen. Ask him to help you see his work in your and others' lives. Ask him to help you trust him. The Lord who sent us Jesus wants you to have eyes of faith to see!

God of Justice
(working with Tamar and Judah)

Judah [was] the father of Perez and Zerah, whose mother was
Tamar. . . .   —Matthew 1:3

Women in Old Testament times often didn't have a lot of options. In that patriarchal culture, a woman without a husband or son was in a precarious situation. The story of Tamar, a widow, is at times sordid and sad. It is also a story in which the men in her life should have acted responsibly for her well-being, but did not. So she took matters into her own hands and pretended to be a prostitute in order to have a rightful heir. We might think that such an action would be condemned, but her widower father-in-law, who actually became the father of her twins, realized that his mistreatment of her was the reason for her actions. When he recognized that he was responsible, he said she was more righteous than he (see Gen. 38).

Sometimes we find ourselves in messes of our own making, and sometimes our misfortunes are brought about by others. Either way, when we turn to God, he is available to bring comfort and hope in distress. God always has concern for those who are vulnerable and mistreated.

If today you find yourself being treated unjustly, you can be certain that God knows and cares. Pray that the one who sees all will come to your aid. And if you are in a position to help someone who is being treated unjustly, know that when you help, you are sharing the "heart" of God.

God of the "Outsider"
(working with Ruth and Boaz)

"Look," said Naomi, "your sister-in-law is going back to her people and her gods. Go back with her." But Ruth replied, "Don't urge me to leave you or to turn back from you. Where you go I will go, and where you stay I will stay. Your people will be my people and your God my God."
                                                            —Ruth 1:15-16

Ruth, another woman mentioned in the genealogy of Jesus (Matt. 1:5), lived in the period of the judges, a difficult time in Jewish history. A widow from the nation of Moab (present-day Jordan), Ruth took a tremendous risk in returning to the town of Bethlehem with her Jewish mother-in-law, Naomi. By doing that, Ruth reduced her chances of ever marrying again and securing a better future for herself.

But God was watching over Ruth, and he rewarded her care for Naomi by providing a husband for her. Perhaps because his own mother (Rahab—see Josh. 2; 6:24-25; Matt. 1:5) was an "outsider," Boaz was open to marrying a Moabite woman. He saw in Ruth a person willing to sacrifice for Naomi. Ruth had worked hard to help Naomi and had been willing to listen to her counsel.

The story of Ruth is one in which we can see God working behind the scenes in people's lives. They make their individual choices, but at the same time God is working to provide and bring about surprising outcomes.

Some teachers say the book of Ruth was written to give a history of King David, since Ruth was his great-grandmother. Others say it was written to help the Israelites realize that, in his plan to save the world, God could include people who had been their enemies (see Num. 22-25; Judg. 3). We might add that the book of Ruth also tells the heartwarming story of one of the women in Jesus' genealogy.

As you think about Ruth today, think about how God has included you. Recall the times you realized he was working behind the scenes in your life. Also, remember that God often includes "outsiders" and that we should look for ways to always welcome and include everyone, whatever their background.

God of Forgiveness
(working with David and Bathsheba)
One evening David got up from his bed and walked around on the roof of the palace. From the roof he saw a woman bathing. The woman was very beautiful, and David sent someone to find out about her. The man said, "She is Bathsheba, the daughter of Eliam and the wife of Uriah the Hittite."   —2 Samuel 11:2-3

In the story of David and his adultery with Bathsheba, we see a person who has a close relationship with God make one bad choice after another, greatly harming himself and those around him. For David, it began with a look that led to adultery, an unwanted pregnancy, a cover-up that failed, a murder, and the death of his infant son (2 Sam. 11-12).

Perhaps the most surprising part occurs after David arranges to have Bath-sheba's husband come home from fighting so that he can be with his wife and it will look like Uriah is the father of the child. But Uriah has more integrity than David at this point. He refuses to go home and make love to his wife while his commander and fellow soldiers endure hardships on the battlefront.

David is frustrated and finally sends Uriah back to the front, carrying a message that tells his commander to position him in such a way that he is killed in the next battle. How could David, once a great military leader who cared about and protected his soldiers, come to a point where he has one of his men killed?

Still, God was working in David's life and would keep his promises (see 2 Sam. 7). Through the prophet Nathan, God made clear to David that he had sinned. And David came to his senses and experienced God's great mercy and forgiveness (see Ps. 32; 51).

Today this story warns us that even those who are close to God can fall into great sin. If you are mired in a pattern of sin, ask God to help you change. Admit you cannot do it by yourself. If you are thinking of making a wrong choice, cry out to God and perhaps ask another person to help you keep from doing what will be harmful to you and others.

But if you have already made wrong choices—and we all do—this story also reminds us that there is forgiveness, no matter how great the sin. God fully forgave David when he repented, and he will do the same for you.

God of the Humble
(working with Mary and Joseph)

Mary said: "My soul glorifies the Lord and my spirit rejoices in God my Savior, for he has been mindful of the humble state of his servant. From now on all generations will call me blessed, for the Mighty One has done great things for me—holy is his name."

—Luke 1:46-49

God could have used a royal princess to be the mother of his Son, but instead he chose a young virgin from humble circumstances to be the one who would give birth to Jesus. God could have used a rich, influential man to be Jesus' adoptive father, but instead he used a hardworking carpenter from a small town in Galilee (Luke 2:4; Matt. 13:55).

As we listen to Mary's words in the first chapter of Luke, we can sense her wonder and even confusion about what was happening to her. After all, it took an angel to explain things, and even then it was hard to believe! It also took an angel to convince Joseph that Mary was not pregnant by a man. But they believed, and God was pleased to work through them.

Mary, "the mother of Jesus," is the final woman to be mentioned in the genealogy of Matthew (Matt. 1:16). Can you imagine what it must have been like for Mary to have God work in her this way? No one else has ever experienced what she went through. Luke 2:19 tells us later, "Mary treasured up all these things and pondered them in her heart." Of course, there would be dark days ahead, and she would witness the horrible crucifixion of her son decades later. But Mary would always know she was the one God chose to be the mother of Jesus. And she was humble.

This Christmas season, what are you "pondering" in your heart? What are some "great" things God has done for you? Make a mental list or write down some of the things that have happened in your life that clearly indicate God is at work. Then remember as you look forward to the future how God uses the humble to accomplish his purposes, no matter what the circumstances. Follow Mary's lead when the angel told her what would happen and she said, "I am the Lord's servant. . . . May your word to me be fulfilled" (Luke 1:38).

Lesson 3
A Scandal? A Stable? Shepherds?

Matthew 1:18-25; Luke 2:1-20

In this lesson we examine the story of Jesus' birth and the unusual circumstances and happenings that surrounded it. With Mary and Joseph, along with countless believers throughout the centuries, we discover the uncommon wonder of the most important birth in history.

Plan ahead to celebrate! *For a time of celebration at the end of this study, see suggestions at the beginning of lesson 5. (If you won't have time to do lesson 5, you may want to have a party during your next session, in connection with lesson 4.)*

Opener (optional)
What are your expectations from the Lord in this season?

EPISODE 1

Matthew 1:18-21
1. Discuss the situation of Mary's pregnancy and how it affected both Mary and Joseph.

To think about as you discuss . . .
- what happened to Mary
- Joseph's reactions
- the angel's message
- the child's identity (as Savior, Messiah; see glossary)

Advent Wreath (Optional)

————

Week Three—Joy
Read: Luke 2:20

We light this third candle of Advent remembering the **joy** of the shepherds when they heard the good news that a savior had been born and they found the baby, just as the angel had told them.

Group prayer: We praise and glorify you, O God, like the shepherds did so long ago. Thank you for this Christmastime, when we praise you for all you have done through Christ, our Savior. Lead us to share the good news with great joy! In Jesus, Amen.

Christmas carol: "Go, Tell It on the Mountain"

Engaged or Married?

What does it mean that Mary and Joseph were "pledged to be married" (Matt. 1:18)? The *NIV Study Bible* offers a helpful explanation: "There were no sexual relations during a Jewish betrothal period, but it was a much more binding relationship than a modern engagement and could be broken only by divorce (see v. 19). In Deuteronomy 22:24 a betrothed woman is called a 'wife,' though the preceding verse speaks of her as being 'pledged to be married.' Matthew uses the terms 'husband' (v. 19) and 'wife' (v. 24) of Joseph and Mary before they were married." See also the angel's statement in Matthew 1:20. *Note:* Some translations use the word "know" in Matthew 1:25 to refer to having sexual relations.

Matthew 1:22-23

2. How does Matthew show that Jesus' birth fulfills a promise?

To think about as you discuss . . .

- the announcement through the prophet (see Isa. 7:14)
- the meaning of the name *Immanuel*

Matthew 1:24-25

3. What is Joseph's response to the angel?

To think about as you discuss . . .

- what this tells us about Joseph
- the significance of his not having sexual relations with Mary till she gave birth

Sculpture of virgin Mary at Barcelona Cathedral

More to Think About

- Considering the prophecy of Isaiah 7:14, do you think anyone expected there would be a virgin birth? Why or why not? (If you have time, examine the story in which Isaiah's prophecy takes place, and see notes in the *NIV Study Bible* or another helpful resource.)

Luke 2:1-7

4. What causes Joseph and Mary to travel to Bethlehem?

To think about as you discuss . . .

- why it had to be Bethlehem
- what would make the travel difficult

Cows eating from a manger

5. When and where does Mary give birth?

To think about as you discuss . . .

- the location and circumstances
- other details Luke mentions

6. Does this seem like a fitting birthplace for a king? Why or why not?

To think about as you discuss . . .

- the humble circumstances of Jesus' birth
- God's care and concern for people who are disadvantaged
- God's call for all to be humble

A Little Town Rich in History

Bethlehem was indeed little, as described in a popular Christmas carol, but it was rich in Jewish history. The story of Ruth takes place there (Ruth 1:1, 19), and her great-grandson, King David of Israel, was born and raised there. In later times it became known as "the town of David" (Luke 2:4, 11). David probably watched sheep in the same fields as the shepherds who were visited by angels on the night of Jesus' birth (Luke 2:8-14). The name *Bethlehem* means "house of bread," so it's a fitting name for an agricultural town. In earlier times the town was known as Ephrath (Gen. 35:16; Ruth 1:2). Rachel, the beloved wife of Jacob the patriarch of Israel, died giving birth to Benjamin on the way there, and she was buried nearby (Gen. 35:16-19). The prophet Micah, calling it "Bethlehem Ephrathah," said the Messiah would come from there (Mic. 5:2; see Matt. 2:6), and it is the town in which Jesus was born (Luke 2:4, 6-7).

EPISODE 2

Luke 2:8-9

7. Where are the shepherds when Jesus is born, and what are they doing?

To think about as you discuss . . .

- the description of the location
- some of the dangers they would have faced (see John 10:11-13)

8. What do the shepherds see, and how do they react? Why?

To think about as you discuss . . .

- what "the glory of the Lord" looked like
- how you might have reacted

Luke 2:10-12

9. What news do the shepherds hear, and what does it mean?

To think about as you discuss . . .

- the specific message
- who will be affected by this news
- why this is "good news"

Why Shepherds?

Though we may romanticize them today, shepherds were not highly respected in Jesus' day. Since they spent so much time out in the fields with their sheep, they often could not observe Jewish ceremonial laws. Their sheep, on the other hand, were prized for the many sacrifices needed at the temple in Jerusalem, about 5 miles (8 km) away from Bethlehem. Scholars add that in Jesus' day shepherds were thought to be so unreliable they could not testify in a court of law. **What does this tell us about God's choice to have them announce the birth of Jesus?** (Consider again the humble circumstances of Jesus' birth—Luke 2:7. See also Luke 1:46-55; 1 Cor. 1:26-31.)

In Israel's past history, however, shepherds and sheep were a common theme in the culture and in Scripture. Many significant people in the Bible were shepherds. Abraham and his family had sheep. Moses was a shepherd, and so were King David and the prophet Amos.

In the Old Testament, God is often described as a shepherd, perhaps most famously in Psalm 23, written by David. The leaders of Israel were also referred to as shepherds (Jer. 23:1-6; Ezek. 34; Zech. 10:2-3), including the promised ruler from Bethlehem (Mic. 5:2-4).

Jesus often used the theme of sheep and shepherds to explain spiritual truths (Luke 15:1-7; John 10), and he referred to himself as "the good shepherd" (John 10:11).

Luke 2:13-15

10. What do the shepherds see next, and what do they decide to do?

To think about as you discuss . . .

- what "the heavenly host" is (see box) and how that would affect the shepherds (see Josh. 5:13-15)
- what convinces them to go and see what they have heard about

What does this mean to me?

- Most of the Christmas art portraying the angels in this story shows them in the sky. From the text, though, it seems they could have surrounded the shepherds at ground level (Luke 2:9, 13). How do you think you would have felt if you could see the hosts of heaven standing around you (see Josh. 5:13-15; 2 Kings 6:17)? Have you had an experience of being overwhelmed with God's glory or an awareness of his presence? If so, what was that like for you?

Luke 2:16-20

11. What do the shepherds find in Bethlehem, and how do they and others respond?

To think about as you discuss . . .

- how they know they have found the right child
- why people believe their story
- their reaction to what they have experienced that night

> The word "angel" in Luke 2:9 comes from the Greek ἄγγελος (angelos), which means "messenger." In the Bible, angels are described as great supernatural beings created by God to do his will. According to the *Baker Encyclopedia of the Bible,* the "heavenly host" described in Luke 2:13 is a reference to "the heavenly powers and angels that act at the Lord's command." See also **glossary**.

12. What would Mary treasure up and ponder in her heart?

To think about as you discuss . . .

- the story the shepherds told her
- all she had experienced up to this point
- the unlikely, unusual events surrounding this birth, and the reason for them

What does this mean to me?

- How has this lesson affected the way you look at the Christmas story?

More to Think About

- During the time of Christ, both shepherds and women were not believed to be reliable witnesses. Consider that Jesus' birth was first announced to shepherds and that his resurrection was first announced to women (see Matt. 28; Mark 16; Luke 24; John 20). What do these facts tell us about God?

- Many people have related personal stories about visits by angels. If you have time, share a couple of those. How did they reveal God or God's care to people?

- As you consider Jesus coming to our earth to enter into our experience, how does that affect the way you view God? (See John 1:14; Heb. 2:14-18; 4:14-16.)

Explore!

- Study the prophecy in Ezekiel 34 about shepherds and sheep, and read Jesus' words about sheep and shepherds in John 10.
- Listen to sections of Handel's *Messiah* on shepherds and sheep. Downloads are available at www.youtube.com (search "Messiah shepherd" and "Messiah sheep").
- Read *A Shepherd Looks at Psalm 23* by W. Phillip Keller, available in several editions at www.amazon.com.
- Take some time with family and friends to view the movie *The Nativity Story* (New Line, 2006), available at most video outlets—a thoughtful adaptation that explores the struggles of Mary and Joseph as God calls them to bear and raise the Savior of the world (Messiah) in their family. Afterward, ask yourselves some questions like these:
  —In what ways is the story faithful to the biblical text?
  —In what ways are the interpretations helpful? In what ways not?
- **Craft idea!** To have a daily reminder of God's love and care for you, construct an easy-to-make refrigerator magnet. (Materials needed: 3" x 5" heavy card stock, craft paper, glue, magnetic backing or clear magnetic frame, printed copy of Psalm 23.)
  —Make a printed copy of Psalm 23, either by hand or on a computer. Finished size should be about 2.5 x 4.5 inches (6.4 x 11.5 cm).
  —Cover the card stock in craft paper and trim.
  —Glue Psalm 23 sheet onto covered cardstock.
  —Slide card into magnetic frame or attach magnetic backing to back of card.

Break Away (at-home readings)

A Shepherd's Psalm

The LORD is my shepherd, I lack nothing. He makes me lie down in green pastures, he leads me beside quiet waters, he refreshes my soul.   —Psalm 23:1-3

Psalm 23 is the best known psalm and perhaps the best-known passage in all of Scripture. Why do you think it's so well known and loved by so many people around the world?

Read this short psalm in your Bible and think about David's experiences as a shepherd and how that might have affected what he wrote. What words of comfort do you find in these verses?

In this Advent season, what needs do you have? Are you in need of some "green pastures" and "quiet waters"? From what "enemies" do you need protection? Use the inspired words of David to provide spiritual refreshment and comfort to your soul.

After you talk about these things with God, ask him to empower you by his Spirit so that you can look back at them without fear and see his hand at work in your life.

He Will Tend His Flock

He tends his flock like a shepherd: He gathers the lambs in his arms and carries them close to his heart; he gently leads those that have young.   —Isaiah 40:11

Sometimes people say that the God of the Old Testament is not as loving as the God of the New Testament. This verse shows that perspective simply is not true. The same God reveals himself in both the Old and New Testaments. This verse from the prophecy of Isaiah describes God in the most strong and yet loving terms.

Think about a shepherd gathering lambs in his arms and holding them close to his heart. The prophet is describing this shepherd as one who "breaks the power of evil with his strong 'arm,' and 'like a shepherd' gathers up the broken in his gentle 'arms'" (John Oswalt, *NIV Isaiah Application Commentary*). All who are willing to be like sheep and follow their Shepherd will experience the tender closeness described here by Isaiah.

A beautiful duet from Handel's *Messiah* is based on this verse ("He shall feed his flock"). If you have the opportunity, listen to this musical piece (available on www.youtube.com; search "Messiah He shall feed") and imagine God as your Shepherd gently guiding you.

Sheep Without a Shepherd

When he saw the crowds, he had compassion on them, because they were harassed and helpless, like sheep without a shepherd.

—Matthew 9:36

Many places in the Bible that refer to sheep and shepherds highlight the predicament of sheep when they are alone. When Jesus saw crowds of people during his ministry, they reminded him of sheep without a shepherd. As you read this verse from Matthew, perhaps you don't see yourself as helpless. But during this busy season of Christmas, you may well identify with the word *harassed*—or at least *harried* and *hurried*.

Sheep are not intelligent enough to understand potential dangers around them, so they need the constant watch of their shepherd. When we, like sheep, choose to wander off and "go it alone" without God, we put ourselves in danger—perhaps not physically, but certainly spiritually. The people whom Jesus observed probably did not realize their predicament, but Jesus, with compassion, longed to be their Shepherd and guide. He also enlisted the help of his disciples and sent them out to help people in their spiritual need (Matt. 9:37-10:42).

At this Christmastime, ask God to guide you in all you plan to do. Ask him also to help you reach out to others with Christ's compassion for the physical and spiritual well-being of everyone around you.

A Life-Giving Shepherd

"I am the good shepherd. The good shepherd lays down his life for the sheep."

—John 10:11

We all, like sheep, have gone astray, each of us has turned to our own way; and the Lord has laid on him the iniquity of us all.

—Isaiah 53:6

Jesus not only says he is the kind of shepherd who will care for his sheep; he also goes so far as to give up his life for them. That's what he did by dying on the cross for our sins. In the greatest transaction of human history, Jesus took all our sins on himself so that we can be forgiven and counted acceptable to God.

As sheep, we have to recognize that we have gone astray and continue to do so. What does "going astray" look like? In his book *The Reason for God*, Tim Keller summarizes the Danish philosopher Søren Kierkegaard's definition of sin when he writes, "Sin is not simply doing bad things, but putting good things in the place of God. So the only solution is not simply to change our behavior, but to reorient and center the entire heart and life on God."

At this holiday time it's important to remember that when we expect other people or things to fulfill what only God can, they will fail us. The "God-shaped vacuum in the heart of every person," as Blaise Pascal called it, can only be filled by the one who will supply not all we may want, but all we truly need.

The God of Peace

Now may the God of peace, who through the blood of the eternal covenant brought back from the dead our Lord Jesus, that great Shepherd of the sheep, equip you with everything good for doing his will, and may he work in us what is pleasing to him, through Jesus Christ, to whom be glory for ever and ever. Amen.

—Hebrews 13:20-21

Peace on earth is often talked about at Christmas. In the book of Hebrews we are told that the God we worship is a God of peace who will equip us to do what is good.

In this passage Jesus is again referred to as the "great Shepherd of the sheep."

Because Jesus has been brought back to life—after dying on the cross for our sins—we can have the confidence that his finished work has saved us to live a meaningful new life right now.

Because he has returned to life, we can have the confidence that someday when we die, we also will be brought back to life.

Because he has given us this great gift, we can bring him glory in the way we live our lives this Christmas season.

43

Lesson 4
Don't Be Afraid: Good News and Peace!

Luke 2:8-14

On the night of Christ's birth, a multitude of angels burst forth in glorious light with a song of hope. To this world bathed in darkness, they brought the good news that God had sent his Son to be the light of the world, announcing peace on earth and favor to people everywhere.

Peace on earth is not just a Christmas catchphrase; it's been the heart's cry of people for millennia. What really is peace on earth?

> **Celebrate!** For a time of celebration at the end of this study, see suggestions at the beginning of the next lesson. (If you won't have time to do lesson 5, you may want to have a party during this session.)

Opener (optional)

If you had all the resources and skills to do one thing that would make the world a better place this Christmas, what would that be?

Luke 2:8-12

To begin, pick up again on your discussion about angels from lesson 3.

1. What would that night have been like for the shepherds?
To think about as you discuss . . .

- the monotony of a routine night watching sheep
- the unexpectedness of the angel's appearance, and the terror and wonder that would go with it
- the relationship between being humble and having faith

Advent Wreath (Optional)

Week Four—Peace
Read: Luke 2:14

We light this fourth candle of Advent remembering the **peace** the angels announced.

Group prayer: Our Father, thank you for sending your Son, Jesus, the "Prince of Peace," so that we can have peace with you and the peace of new life through your Spirit in us, that we can share with others. Amen.

Christmas carol: "Hark! The Herald Angels Sing"

"Heaven is my throne, and the earth is my footstool. . . . Has not my hand made all these things . . . ?" declares the LORD. *"These are the ones I look on with favor: those who are humble and contrite in spirit, and who tremble at my word."*
—Isaiah 66:1-2

2. Why was it important that Jesus' birth be announced by angels?

To think about as you discuss . . .

- who Jesus is
- how the angels' visit would make the message believable

3. The angel told the shepherds that the good news was for "all people." Why might that be a surprise?

To think about as you discuss . . .

- recall your earlier discussion of good news in lesson 3
- the Jews' role as God's specially chosen people (Ex. 6:7; Deut. 26:16-19; Jer. 31:33)
- the original purpose God had in making them into his people (Gen. 12:2-3; John 4:21-24; 10:14-16)

What does this mean to me?

- In what ways does this promise encourage you? How can it help all of us to encourage others?

4. When the multitude of angels appears, they give glory to God. What has God done in your life for which you can give glory to him this Christmas season?

Luke 2:13-14

5. What did the angels mean by the word "peace"? How does this differ from political "peace"?

To think about as you discuss . . .

- the kind of peace that God promises in this life (Rom. 5:1-11; Eph. 2:14-22; Phil. 4:4-9)
- whether political peace is possible without having God's peace

6. What are some ways in which people try to find peace for themselves?

What does this mean to me?

- Where in your life do you need to make peace with God?

- How can making peace with God help you to make peace with others?

Why is a dove often used as a symbol of peace?

For Christians, the dove is not only a reminder of the bird that Noah released from the ark and that returned with an olive leaf (Gen. 8:10-11), but the dove is also a symbol of the Holy Spirit, which "descended on [Jesus] in bodily form, like a dove" when he was baptized (Luke 3:22; see John 1:32-34). God made peace with sinners through the sacrifice of his Son (Rom. 5:1-11), who has become "our peace" (Eph. 2:14-22). All who believe this message of salvation are filled with the Holy Spirit (Acts 2:38-39) and have peace with God (Phil. 4:4-9).

7. What does it mean to have God's favor rest on you?

To think about as you discuss . . .

- the word *favor* can mean "goodwill, kindly intent, benevolence"
- the relationship between God's favor and peace—and *grace* (see glossary)

8. The coming of Christ (Messiah) was the fulfillment of promises given many centuries earlier. Today we wait for Christ's second coming. How is our situation today similar? How is it different?

To think about as you discuss . . .

- the Jews' longing for a savior to come and deliver them
- the promises they received, along with traditions and a history of God's faithfulness to them (see Ps. 105-106; 135-136)
- our desire to live fully with God in a new heaven and earth (Isa. 65:17-25; Rev. 21-22)
- our need for patience as we wait, and why (see 2 Pet. 3:8-13)
- how this connects to our involvement in spreading the good news and the peace of God
- experiences you've had in waiting for answers to prayer (give examples of answers you expected, and answers you did not expect)

Why are there four candles around the Advent wreath? One tradition says that the four candles symbolize the **four hundred years of waiting** between the last word from the Old Testament prophet Malachi and the birth of Christ.

More to Think About

- As Christians, we have peace with God. As a response to this wonderful gift, what are some ways you can bring this peace into the world around you?

- Remembering all the things God has done for you is an important part of growing in faith. By sending Christ to us, God has offered us grace and peace. What other things has God done for you in the past few weeks/months? Make a list. As you do, thank him for each one.

- Is there someone you need to make peace with? If so, the Christmas season is the perfect time to do it. Can you make a phone call, send a Christmas card, make and deliver some treats? Sometimes it's too late to make peace face to face. If that's the case, talk it over with God. It's never too late to ask or give forgiveness.

Explore!

- Another beautiful song from Handel's *Messiah* is "Glory to God," based on the angels' song in Luke 2:14. Take a few minutes to listen to a recording of it (available on www.youtube.com; search "Messiah Glory to God"), and reflect on the astonishing message delivered to the shepherds that cold, dark night long ago: the glorious Lord of heaven and earth came to live among us to extend peace to all who will receive it.
- Ministries and organizations that promote social justice are also promoting peace in the lives of people in need. The Christmas season is a wonderful time to get involved in short-term projects. Here are a few ideas:

   Free a Family helps you "assist a child and the whole village that is raising him at the same time! . . . [It] helps children overcome poverty through community programs for parents and caregivers in agriculture, health, nutrition, literacy, and more." For more information on this and other opportunities through World Renew, visit www.worldrenew.net.

Angel Tree: A program through Prison Fellowship that "seeks to reconcile prisoners and their families to God and to each other through the delivery of Christmas gifts and the gospel message." Through angel tree you can either purchase a gift for a child of a prison inmate, or you can get your whole church group together to sponsor several children. Information is available at www.angeltree.org.

Operation Christmas Child: A program through Samaritan's Purse in which you pack a shoebox full of small gifts and toys for a child in a third world nation. "Since 1970, Samaritan's Purse has helped meet needs of people who are victims of war, poverty, natural disaster, disease, and famine with the purpose of sharing God's love through his Son, Jesus Christ." Information is available at www.samaritanspurse.org under "What We Do."

- **Craft idea!** Make dove-shaped Christmas gift tags or ornaments to remember the peace that God offers you through the gift of his Holy Spirit. Trace the template provided here and transfer it onto cardstock or similar stiff paper. Cut out the dove, and make a hole for a ribbon. Cover one side in a thin layer of craft glue. Sprinkle glitter over the glue, shake off excess. For tags: Allow glue and glitter to dry before lacing ribbon through hole. For ornaments: Allow one side to dry before applying glue and glitter to the other side. When completely dry, lace a ribbon through the hole and hang.

Break Away (at-home readings)

A Peace-filled Mind

You will keep in perfect peace those whose minds are steadfast, because they trust in you. Trust in the LORD forever, for the LORD, the LORD himself, is the Rock eternal.   —Isaiah 26:3-4

God promises peace (*perfect* peace!) to those whose minds are set on trusting him. Have you ever tried to trust in God but found yourself slipping away into worry and fear? Why is trusting God so difficult sometimes?

In Romans 8 the apostle Paul talks about two natures warring inside each of us—our sinful (greedy, worrying, selfish) nature and the part of us that loves God and wants to serve him. Paul explains the only solution to this internal struggle: "You, however, are controlled not by the sinful nature but are in the realm of the Spirit . . ." (Rom. 8:9). In a way like Dorothy in *The Wizard of Oz*, whose ruby slippers had the power to bring her home, we have had the solution to our problem all along. We have the Holy Spirit living in us. He is able to help us trust God and be steadfast (firm, faithful).

Ask God today to empower you by his Spirit so that you can trust him in every area of your life (work, play, family, education, finances, social, etc.). If you have been in the habit of giving way to fear and worry, pray for forgiveness and for the power to be steadfast. Then thank God that his desire for you is that you have peace. Thank him for making the way to peace possible and for giving you the power to have his peace in Christ through the Holy Spirit.

Peace in Times of Change

The Lord appeared to [Isaac] and said, "I am the God of your father Abraham. Do not be afraid, for I am with you; I will bless you and will increase the number of your descendants. . . ."   —Genesis 26:24

If the shepherds needed comforting from the angel who appeared to them (Luke 2:9), Isaac needed more. Isaac had an encounter with God himself! God came to Isaac at a very difficult time in his life: he was afraid a local king would kill him and take his wife; he was pursued by quarreling herds-men who took over every well he dug (Gen. 26). Isaac's life was in turmoil.

Does your life feel like it's in turmoil? Have you been in a place where you have had to deal with more change and challenge than you could handle? God's promise to Isaac is for you as well: "Do not be afraid, for I am with you." Meditate on that promise for a moment. What does it mean to you?

"God is not human, that he should lie [or] . . . change his mind. . . . Does he promise and not fulfill?" (Num. 23:19). "Every good and perfect gift is from above, coming down from the Father of the heavenly lights, who does not change like shifting shadows" (James 1:17).

God does not change. Is that a comfort to you this Christmas season? Think of five ways in which God has not changed in his love for you. Write them down, and then go back over them and thank him for each one.

Peace About "Small" Things

"Look at the birds of the air; they do not sow or reap or store away in barns, and yet your heavenly Father feeds them. Are you not much more valuable than they?"   —Matthew 6:26

The people in Jesus' day had to work hard to survive. Their lives were especially difficult under the political system of the Roman Empire. No one looked out for the little guy—no one except God.

Have there been times in your life when you have felt insignificant? Have you faced problems that you have thought are too small for God to bother with? Do you wonder if God really cares about the details in your life? Our Lord assures us that God watches over even tiny creatures and that we are far more valuable to him than they are!

Scripture says that God loves and tends all he has made, no matter how insignificant it might seem to us. Every single person is well within the scope of his care. Meditate on these words from Psalm 139:1-3: "You have searched me, Lord, and you know me. You know when I sit and when I rise; you perceive my thoughts from afar. You discern my going out and my lying down; you are familiar with all my ways."

You can be at peace knowing that you are not nameless and faceless to God. Your problems and fears are not unknown to him. Take a few moments to ask God for his help with some of the small details of your life. "Cast your anxiety on him because he cares for you" (1 Pet. 5:7).

Prayers for Peace

"Our God . . . we have no power to face this vast army that is attacking us. We do not know what to do. . . ." —2 Chronicles 20:12

Are there situations or relationships in your life that make you feel like it's pointless to pray about them? Places in your life where it seems impossible to find peace? A cause that you care about that doesn't seem to make much headway in the world?

Jehoshaphat, a great-great-great grandson of David who ruled over God's people (see Matt. 1:8), had an impossible situation one day. The land of Judah was about to be destroyed by a vast army of enemy nations. In his alarm, Jehoshaphat prayed a beautiful prayer of faith, praising God's great power and faithfulness, and closing by saying: "We have no power to face this vast army that is attacking us. We do not know what to do, but our eyes are on you."

Meditate on this prayer for a few moments. It was clear that survival was only possible for Jehoshaphat and God's people if the Lord intervened. Use this prayer as your own and take some time to pray about the things in your life that are impossible without God's intervention. As Jesus himself said, "With God all things are possible" (Matt. 19:26).

(See the next reading for the outcome of Jehoshaphat and his people's situation.)

Praise and Peace

"Do not be afraid or discouraged because of this vast army. For the battle is not yours, but God's. . . . You will not have to fight this battle. Take up your positions; stand firm and see the deliverance the LORD will give you. . . . Do not be afraid; do not be discouraged. Go out to face them . . . and the LORD will be with you." —2 Chronicles 20:15-17

Just like the angel's message to the shepherds (Luke 2:10), God's word to Jehoshaphat begins with the words "Do not be afraid . . ." The king and the terrified inhabitants of Jerusalem needed to hear those words. But would they believe them? Nothing else had changed—there was still a vast army marching toward them.

How do you trust that God's Word is true when everything seems to be falling apart? What do you do?

Jehoshaphat said to his people, "Have faith in the LORD your God and you will be upheld; have faith in his prophets and you will be successful" (2 Chron. 20:20). He then appointed people to sing God's praises as they went out to face the enemy. God caused the enemy armies to become confused and to slaughter one another, and his people were delivered.

While we wait for God to answer, we can decide to worship him. Take a few minutes right now to praise the Lord. Remember his glory and greatness, elaborate creativity, abounding love, and gracious mercy. When your focus is on Christ rather than your overwhelming odds, you can experience the peace that Paul speaks of in Philippians 4:6-7: "Do not be anxious about anything, but in every situation, by prayer and petition, with thanksgiving, present your requests to God. And the peace of God, which transcends all understanding, will guard your hearts and your minds in Christ Jesus."

Though we are not always rescued in the way we might want or expect, we have many promises in Scripture for times of trial. Here are some wonderful ones:

- "I will be with you; I will never leave you nor forsake you. Be strong and courageous. . . ." (Josh. 1:5-6; see Heb. 13:5-6).
- "I know the plans I have for you," declares the LORD, "plans to prosper you and not to harm you, plans to give you hope and a future" (Jer. 29:11).
- "We know that in all things God works for the good of those who love him, who have been called according to his purpose" (Rom. 8:28).
- "[Nothing] in all creation, will be able to separate us from the love of God that is in Christ Jesus our Lord" (Rom. 8:39).

Lesson 5
Celebrate—the King Is Coming!

Isaiah 11:1-9; Revelation 22:12-17

Christmas is almost here. We've been discussing and reflecting on the coming of Christ and the events surrounding his birth—and as the Christmas holiday approaches, it's time to celebrate!

The Advent season climaxes on Christmas Eve. The Christ Candle shines in the middle of the glowing Advent wreath, the singing of favorite carols reverberates through our Lord's churches, and the retelling of the Christmas story comforts our hearts like a visit from an old friend. Like excited children eager to open their gifts, we are full of hope, looking forward. As we anticipate and reflect on Christmas, we also look ahead to the Second Advent, for Christ is coming again—as Lord and King!

Opener (optional)

Is there a particular Christmas that you especially remember? What made it special?

Celebrate Christ's Coming with a Party!

- Have Christmas music playing when people arrive.
- Ahead of time, ask several members of your group to bring a favorite Christmas treat to share. You may want to swap recipes too!
- Swap names for a low-cost gift exchange. Limit the budget and offer a prize for the most creative gift!
- If someone plays a piano or guitar (or with a CD player), sing some Christmas carols together.
- Make plans to do a craft from one of the Explore! sections in this study, or . . .
- Plan an activity such as cookie decorating that you can do together and then make gifts for people who would enjoy being remembered this season.

Advent Wreath (Optional)

Week Five—Christ's Coming
Read: Matthew 1:20-21

We light this last candle of Advent remembering the purpose and blessing of **Christ's coming** to save us from our sins and give us new life forever with God.

Group prayer: Dear Jesus, you have many names: Messiah, Immanuel, Prince of Peace, Savior, and more. Help us this Christmas to celebrate and honor you as King of kings and Lord or lords! Fill us with your life, and help us to share your good news with others. In your name, Amen.

Christmas carol: "Joy to the World!"

Note: This lesson is short so that you and your group can take time to celebrate together!

Isaiah and Revelation

In this lesson we turn again to the book of Isaiah, and we close with a passage from the last book of the Bible: Revelation. Both speak of the return of Christ as the day when everything wrong will be set right and we will live fully in the presence of God our Savior. During this lesson, focus on the way a child anticipates celebrating Christmas. Ask the Lord to help you look forward to his return with that kind of expectant delight.

Isaiah 11:1-3a

1. What are some of the traits of the Messiah noted in these verses?

To think about as you discuss . . .

- the words "shoot," "stump," "roots," "Branch," "fruit"
- how the Holy Spirit is at work in and through this "shoot," or "Branch"

Isaiah 11:3b-5

2. How will Christ judge the world when he returns?

To think about as you discuss . . .

- why at Christmas it is important to reflect on divine justice
- how the Lord's justice is different from human justice
- why God's justice gives us reason to rejoice

What does Jesus say about coming again?

After Jesus rose from the dead, he ascended into heaven (Acts 1:9-11). He also promised to return someday (see Matt. 24:30-25:46; 26:64; Mark 13:26-37; 14:62; Luke 21:27-28; see also Rev. 21:1-7; 22:1-5, 12-21).

Jesse (Isa. 11:1) was "the father of King David" (Matt. 1:6). Recall together the importance of this connection from your study of lesson 2, "Meet the Relatives."

When we speak about wisdom, we are speaking of Christ. When we speak about virtue, we are speaking of Christ. When we speak about justice, we are speaking of Christ. When we speak about peace, we are speaking of Christ. When we speak about truth and life and redemption, we are speaking of Christ.

—St. Ambrose of Milan (A.D. 339-397)

On that day we will see our Savior face to face, sacrificed Lamb and triumphant King, just and gracious.

He will set all things right, judge evil, and condemn the wicked.

We face that day without fear, for the Judge is our Savior, whose shed blood declares us righteous.

We live confidently, anticipating his coming, offering him our daily lives—our acts of kindness, our loyalty, and our love—knowing that he will weave even our sins and sorrows into his sovereign purpose.

Come, Lord Jesus, come.

—*Our World Belongs to God: A Contemporary Testimony,* para. 57

Isaiah 11:6-9

3. What images in these verses stand out in your mind or affect you most? Why?

To think about as you discuss . . .

- how unity, love, and peace are portrayed
- what it will be like to live in a place like this

A version of *The Peaceable Kingdom* by Edward Hicks (1780-1849), based on Isaiah 11:1-9.

What does this mean to me?

- When Christ returns, everything will be set right. What are your thoughts about that? How does this affect your relationship with God?

Revelation 22:12-17

4. When does Christ say he will return? What does this mean to you?

To think about as you discuss . . .

- how we are called to live as we await his return
- how God views time (see 2 Peter 3:8-9, at right)

> But do not forget this one thing, dear friends: With the Lord a day is like a thousand years, and a thousand years are like a day. The Lord is not slow in keeping his promise, as some understand slowness. He is patient with you, not wanting anyone to perish, but everyone to come to repentance.—2 Peter 3:8-9

5. How can reflecting on the second coming of Christ enrich your celebration of Christmas this year?

A Thought to Consider

Maybe this study has helped you come to a new understanding of Jesus. You may feel prompted to respond to what you've learned. For thousands of years, people have done this by devoting their lives to Christ. You can do that by telling God you're sorry for your sins and by asking him to forgive you and to live within you. Thank the Lord for his mercy, his forgiveness, and his love for you. Then ask your group leader and others to help you connect with the local church and become a part of it so that you can join with others who are, like you, devoted to following Christ.

More to Think About

- Think about your level of anticipation for the second coming of Jesus. Do you need to change or adjust anything in your life to live with more anticipation for the coming King? If so, what? How?

Explore!

- Another beautiful piece in Handel's *Messiah* is the "Hallelujah Chorus." A recording of this outpouring of praise to God is available at www.youtube.com (search "Messiah Hallelujah Chorus").

- Pick up *The Last Battle*, the final book in C. S. Lewis's *Chronicles of Narnia,* for a vivid story of the return of Aslan, the Christ figure in the series. A quick and delightful read, this book uses the power of metaphor to help build your anticipation and longing for the return of Christ to this world. As Lucy, one of the characters who visits Narnia from our world, puts it, "Yes . . . in our world too, a Stable once had something inside it that was bigger than our whole world."

- **Craft idea!** Consider how we praise God in this season of the year and how we can truly praise our Creator and Savior all year long. In response, make your own book of praises. *Materials:* 1 sheet of 8.5 x 11 card stock, 10 sheets of 8.5 x 11 paper, gift wrap or decorative paper, double-sided tape or a glue stick, paper cutter, stapler, ruler, pencil, bone folder, 2 binder clips.
  - Cut card stock and 8.5 x 11 paper in half with paper cutter.
  - Sandwich paper between the two pieces of card stock and line edges up. Fasten with binder clips along one side, and then staple the pages together about 1/8 in. (3.2 mm) from the edge.
  - Cut a piece of gift wrap or decorative paper slightly larger than your book, and fold in half with bone folder. Insert book, pressing against the fold to make spine. Secure paper to book with double-sided tape (or use glue stick).
  - Trim edges of decorative paper or gift wrap neatly to the edges of the cardstock.
  - Over the next year, use this little book as a place to record what God has done for you and how you are responding in praise.

Break Away (at-home readings)

Joy to the World!

Joy to the world! The Lord is come: Let earth receive her King!
Let every heart prepare him room, and heaven and nature sing,
and heaven and nature sing, and heaven, and heaven and nature
sing!   —Isaac Watts (1719)

This hymn is based on Psalm 98: "Shout for joy to the Lord, all the earth,
burst into jubilant song with music. . . . Let the sea resound, and everything
in it, the world, and all who live in it. Let the rivers clap their hands, let the
mountains sing together for joy; let them sing before the Lord, for he comes
to judge the earth. He will judge the world in righteousness and the peoples
with equity" (vv. 4-9).

Though we sing this hymn at Christmastime, it was not written as a Christmas song. It was written about the Second Advent of Christ—the day he
will come again and rule in righteousness forever. What a wonderful song to
sing as we anticipate both the Christmas season and the return of our King!

Meditate for a few moments on the picture of the whole earth—people and
all of nature—worshiping God. What does that look like? What sounds do
you hear? How do you think you will be feeling when this happens?

If you know the song "Joy to the World!" take some time right now to sing it
to the Lord. It doesn't matter what you think you sound like; God delights in
your song of praise.

Rejoice today that your King came as a baby, and that he sacrificed his
life so you can have peace with God. Rejoice that he hears and helps you.
Rejoice that he is coming again in power and glory to set all things right.
Rejoice and sing with songs of praise!

Come, Thou Long-Expected Jesus

Come, thou long-expected Jesus, born to set thy people free;
from our fears and sins release us, let us find our rest in thee.
Israel's strength and consolation, hope of all the earth thou art:
dear desire of every nation, joy of every longing heart.

—Charles Wesley (1744)

When Christ came to live among us, one of his purposes was to change the future of humanity. He came to fulfill ancient prophecies, to be the Messiah of his people, to break the power of sin and death so that anyone who believes in him can be saved from an eternity apart from God. When he returns again, he will rule the nations, and every knee will bow and every tongue will confess that he is Lord (Phil. 2:10-11).

The big picture isn't the only thing he's concerned with, however. As much as he is Israel's strength, Christ is also concerned with your fears and sins. He is the desire of all nations, and he wants to be the joy of your longing heart. Christ is interested in you, and he loves you.

How long has it been since you have told Christ how much you love him? Here are some words that David wrote to express his love for God: "You, God, are my God, earnestly I seek you; I thirst for you, my whole being longs for you, in a dry and parched land where there is no water. . . . Because your love is better than life, my lips will glorify you" (Ps. 63:1-3).

Any of us can make these words our prayer of love to God. How has God shown his love toward you lately? Thank him. What fears and sins do you need to be released from? Ask him for help.

Take a moment to reflect on the picture of the tiny baby lying in a manger. As you do, consider that as much as he came to change the world, he also came to change you.

Hark! The Herald Angels Sing

Hark! The herald angels sing, "Glory to the newborn King;
peace on earth, and mercy mild, God and sinners reconciled!"
Joyful, all ye nations, rise; join the triumph of the skies;
with th' angelic host proclaim, "Christ is born in Bethlehem!"
Hark! The herald angels sing, "Glory to the newborn King!"

—Charles Wesley (1739)

A herald is an official messenger; this hymn speaks of the multitude of messengers (angels) that came straight from the throne room of God. These angels brought the message of peace and favor (grace) with God—because the Savior had been born! As Romans 8:1 puts it, "There is now no condemnation for those who are in Christ Jesus. . . ." There is no sentence of judgment for people who follow Christ—we have a "get out of jail free" card. The punishment we deserve has been taken away!

Are you in need of God's mercy today? Have you done something that you think is unforgivable? Is there a habitual sin that you just can't seem to shake? Don't lose hope—there is no condemnation for those who belong to Christ. He wants you to come to him and pour out your heart, confessing your sins. Whatever they are, he can forgive.

Romans 8 continues with these words (vv. 2-5): "Through Christ Jesus the law of the Spirit who gives life has set you free from the law of sin and death. . . . Those who live in accordance with the Spirit have their minds set on what the Spirit desires."

Do you keep your mind set on the things God desires? Do you spend time in conversation with God, in reading your Bible? Do you avoid places or things that cause you to sin? Do you try in all you do to bring glory to God, "glory to the newborn King"? (See 1 Cor. 10:31; Col. 3:17.) Think about these things. Make up your mind to live in a way that pleases God, and then pray, asking the Holy Spirit to give you the strength to be able to live this way, for Jesus' sake.

O Come, All Ye Faithful

O come, all ye faithful, joyful and triumphant!
O come ye, O come ye to Bethlehem!
Come and behold him, born the King of angels;
O come, let us adore him, O come, let us adore him,
O come, let us adore him, Christ the Lord!   —John F. Wade (1743)

What does it mean to be faithful? It means to be loyal or to be committed to something or someone with your whole heart. A faithful person is someone who can be trusted, who never gives up when the going gets hard.

God is faithful to us. "The Lord is trustworthy in all he promises and faithful in all he does" (Ps. 145:13). One of God's promises is that he gives us his Holy Spirit to transform us, from the inside out, to be more like Christ (John 14:6-17, 26-27; 2 Cor. 3:18). As we daily spend time with God in conversation (prayer), in studying his Word (the Bible), and in thoughtful obedience, we slowly become who God intends us to be. The "fruit of the Spirit" develops in us: "love, joy, peace, patience, kindness, goodness, faithfulness, gentleness and self-control" (Gal. 5:22-23).

How would your life look if you had more love? More joy? More peace? More patience? More kindness? More goodness? More faithfulness? More gentleness? More self-control? Ask God to grow these things in you, to make you more "faithful, joyful and triumphant." As you submit your life more and more to the Lord, as you sacrifice to spend time daily with him, as you obey him more and more, you will be able to look back on your life and see a miraculous transformation. You will look with joy at how God has enabled you to triumph over sin.

Go, Tell It on the Mountain

Go, tell it on the mountain, over the hills and everywhere;
go, tell it on the mountain that Jesus Christ is born.
                              —traditional spiritual, 19th century

This song is a spiritual sung by African American slaves as they toiled and suffered on plantations in the southern United States. Imagine with what passion this song was sung—passion for a God who values all human life equally and calls for justice (righteousness) and *shalom* (peaceful flourishing

62

in the kingdom of God). When we see justice breaking through, shining light into the darkness of human misery, there is reason to rejoice! But in matters calling for justice in this world, there is still a long way to go.

What reasons do you have to rejoice? What has God done in your life that needs to be told?

There are people in your life who need to hear the things God has done for you. People who are living in spiritual darkness need to see a glimmer of hope—hope that there is a God who cares about them. Who are those people in your life? Take a few moments to write down their names.

There are also people living in misery because of injustice: prejudice, racism, unfair labor practices, unjust immigration laws, and more. In what ways can you help? What can you do for people in your community who have to deal with such trouble?

Today, take some time to pray for the people you have been thinking about. In the days ahead, look for opportunities to spend time with them, and commit yourself to being a true friend to them. Ask God to give you wisdom (James 1:5) to help you to bring the good news and the help that people need. Take some time also to reflect on Isaiah 61:1-2, Luke 4:14-21, and Jesus' charge to us in Matthew 25:31-40. Ask the Spirit of God to keep molding you to be more like Christ, the King!

Evaluation Questionnaire

Infuse Bible Studies — Christmas: Light Splits the Night

As you complete this study, please fill out this questionnaire to help us evaluate the effectiveness of our materials. Please be candid. Thank you.

1. Was this a home group _____ or a church-based _____ program?
   What church?

2. Was the study used for
   _____ a community evangelism group?
   _____ a community faith-nurture group?
   _____ a church Bible study group?

3. How would you rate the materials?
   Study Guide _____ excellent _____ very good _____ good _____ fair _____ poor
   Leader's Notes on website _____ excellent _____ very good _____ good _____ fair _____ poor

4. What were the strengths?

5. What were the weaknesses?

6. What would you suggest to improve the material?

7. In general, what was the experience of your group?

Your name (optional) _____

Address _____

_____

8. Other comments: